AUSTRALIAN
QUILTS
THE PEOPLE AND THEIR ART

AUSTRALIAN QUILTS

THE PEOPLE AND THEIR ART

Text by Jan Irvine
Photography by Roger Deckker

THE QUILTERS' GUILD

SIMON SCHUSTER

AUSTRALIA

Acknowledgements

The Quilters' Guild gratefully acknowledges assistance given by the following:

Australia Council, for funding the suitcase exhibitions; Australian Bicentennial Authority's Women '88 program, for continued support of Quilt Australia '88; Coats Semco; Canberra exhibitors; the Wollstonecraft Quilters; Margot Child; Wendy Holland; Alison Muir.

Cover quilt by Trudy Billingsley

AUSTRALIAN QUILTS: THE PEOPLE AND THEIR ART
First published in Australasia in 1989 by
Simon & Schuster Australia
7 Grosvenor Place, Brookvale NSW 2100

A division of Gulf + Western

National Library of Australia
Cataloguing in Publication data

Irvine, Jan.
Australian quilts.

ISBN 0 7318 0080 X (limp).
ISBN 0 7318 0110 5 (cased).

1. Quilting — Australia. 2. Quiltmakers — Australia.
I. Deckker, Roger. II. Quilters' Guild (Australia). III.
Title.

746.46'0994

Designed by Deborah Brash/Brash Design
Typeset in Australia by Savage Type Pty Ltd, Brisbane
Produced by Mandarin Offset in Hong Kong

Foreword

In Australia in recent years, there has been a significant development in exhibitions at the regional level, particularly in the development of opportunities for regional and isolated centres and artists. This, to a great extent, has come about as a result of increased touring of exhibitions.

The Australia Council, the Australian federal government's arts policy and funding body, seeks to encourage development by ensuring that a balanced program of high-quality exhibitions is available throughout Australia and that the work of Australian artists is exhibited nationally and internationally.

'Quilts Covering Australia', a project funded by the Visual Arts/Crafts Board of the Australia Council, is a particularly fine example of an exhibition incorporating innovative and thought-provoking works by forty-three fibre artists from around Australia. Each quilter was commissioned to make a quilt to a standard size, and the resultant quality and diversity of design and technique are outstanding.

Particularly significant is the range of work reflecting both the traditional idioms of quiltmaking in the ornate patterned work, and the more narrative pictorial style that has emerged over recent years. This exhibition is a succinct summary of the way a particular contemporary art practice can draw on its own traditions, and on new styles and stimuli, to continue to generate new forms and new ways of representing what the artist sees. For, regardless of style and format, the important quality in all art is the artist's view of the world, of current and imagined possibilities, and how we can draw on that vision to better understand ourselves and our future.

The Visual Arts/Crafts Board saw in this project a chance to present a spectrum of contemporary quiltmaking to a very wide public audience, and is delighted to have had the opportunity to assist this ambitious project. The project has received enthusiastic support from the participating artists, the general public, the hosting venues and organising bodies. The exhibition and this publication establish a model which can become a widely accepted form for presenting the work of artists to a growing public audience for contemporary art.

Marjorie Johnson
Chair
Visual Arts/Craft Board
Australia Council

Contents

The Quiltmakers

The Suitcase Exhibitions

In 1988 The Quilters' Guild commissioned forty-three quiltmakers from all over Australia to create small quilts that could tour even the remotest parts of the country — and so the 'suitcase exhibitions' were born. The Guild was keen to reach quilters and interested members of communities too small to have any exhibition space large enough to house displays of full-sized quilts. Jan Irvine conceived the idea of an easily transportable exhibition of small quilts, which could be packed into suitcases, along with display modules and any necessary material required to stage it. The exhibition was enthusiastically supported by Guild members and assisted financially by the Australia Council. For five years 'Quilts Covering Australia' will crisscross the continent, covering every state and territory. Sally Evers, one of the contributors, sums up the enthusiasm for the format:

> The idea of quilts travelling the country in suitcases equipped for "instant exhibition" caught my imagination immediately.
>
> The portability and relatively small space required to set up the stands makes it possible to show the quilts far and wide, reaching the widest possible viewing public . . . It seems to me a most delightful way of keeping in touch with quilters wherever they live in our vast country.

The quiltmakers chosen to produce these small works for the exhibition were selected to provide a representative cross-section of styles and techniques. Their work and their words are presented here in *Australian Quilts: The People and Their Art*.

Many of the contributors have been sewing since childhood, often influenced by the needle-work of their mothers. Their introduction to quiltmaking may have come later, but the basic techniques were ingrained. Some of the quiltmakers come from backgrounds in embroidery or a variety of artistic disciplines, so they had already experimented with colour and design on fabric in order to create another layer of texture and meaning. Most quiltmakers, however, have become involved in quilting without any formal training. For many, quiltmaking is a means of expressing their creativity. Beryl Hodges explains the excitement generated:

> It fascinates me that quilting puts creativity within reach of anyone by offering levels of achievement. Trying a traditional pattern allows choice of colour, pattern and inter-relation, while at the other end of the spectrum you can be totally unconventional.

Traditional designs and techniques certainly play an important part in Australian quiltmaking but, like colour and fabric, they can be manipulated to achieve new effects and individual interpretations. Some quiltmakers have entirely dispensed with traditional patterns and use the fabric as a medium for the expression of their visions. Jan Irvine comments:

> You often hear reference to the "quilt as an art form". The demarcation between art and craft is tiresome to me. I believe that personal expression is the point of creative activity, be that a modest qualification or a driving passion in life.

A large number of the quiltmakers have been inspired by the vast palette of colours and fascinating shapes to be discovered in Australia's varied landscape, as well as in its flora and fauna. Others find frequent stimulus in sources as elemental as the changing patterns of light and shade. When not consulting the natural environment, other works of art, from our own and other cultures, can serve as a creative source.

Fabrics, too, can elicit a response. Margot Child sums up the feelings of many quiltmakers when she explains: 'Fabric is very evocative for me. I can conjure up memories of the texture and pattern of certain materials in my past.' Texture, colour and prints all play an important part in the development of a design. Many of the quilters represented in this book are fascinated by the interactions that are formed between coloured and textured pieces of fabric when they are placed next to each other. Jennifer Lewis is one:

> The different textures and colours of the fabrics and the scope for individual design appeal to me. I enjoy the way the personality of the quilter comes through the quilt — their choice of colour and design and the fascinating differences in the results.

This fine collection of small quilts from the 'Quilts Covering Australia' exhibition shows the exciting juxtaposition of styles, colours and techniques that are representative of the highly individual talents and preoccupations of Australian quiltmakers. They demonstrate perfectly the happy union of self expression and artistic challenge that is an integral part of this developing craft.

DIANNE FINNEGAN
President 1986–88
The Quilters' Guild

Sally Evers

● MY FASCINATION IS WITH THE DESIGN PROCESS; A SORT OF PAINTING WITH FABRIC ●

HOBART, TAS Sally was raised in Tasmania. After her marriage to a diplomat, she lived in several countries, eventually settling back in Tasmania. Her influences are drawn from varied sources and expressed in work ranging from pocket-handkerchief wall-hangings to queen-size bed quilts.

I BEGAN QUILTMAKING in 1982. In the beginning I wanted to learn all the techniques involved in making a quilt. I wanted to know about materials, batting, stitching — everything. I started with a practical aim. I wanted to be artistic but my purpose was to make bedcovers for the family.

Now, some thirty-five quilts later, my enthusiasm for the art has not diminished. My fascination is with the design process; a sort of painting with fabric. That is not to say I'm after effects that could more easily be achieved by paint on paper or canvas but rather the effects that preserve and enhance the fabrics themselves. For me, the tactile quality is fundamental and therefore the quilting is an integral part of the design process.

After I married, we lived in different countries and in Canberra before eventually coming back to Tasmania. The artistic traditions of cultures as diverse as ancient Egyptian, African, Chinese and Japanese on the one hand, and modern Western art on the other, have been a constant source of inspiration. I'm particularly interested in the Impressionist, Post-Impressionist and Fauve schools of painting.

I work alone. Ostensibly my ideas come from collected pictures and scribblings. However, a design often comes in a flash, unexpectedly. The concept may need very little refining but the designing doesn't stop until all the pieces are sewn together. Although my work is highly personal, the techniques I employ come from the long tradition of quiltmakers whose work inspired me in the first place.

I have developed an individual style and within that I'm equally at home with wild, exuberant designs or quiet, reflective ones. I like to work with a number of different fabrics, mostly furnishing fabrics because of their greater subtlety. My work is never simply a visual statement. I hope that my use of colour and pattern creates something that sparks the viewer's imagination.

▶ **Cottage Garden**
cottons, polycottons;
machine pieced, hand quilted

Marjorie Coleman

❝I DIDN'T TRY TO BREAK ANY RADICAL NEW GROUND WITH THIS QUILT BUT CONTINUED TO EXPLORE PLANT FORMS AND EXPRESS THEM THROUGH APPLIQUE❞

PERTH, WA Marjorie has developed an individual design style and application in her quiltmaking, born out of her own experience. She draws her imagery from her native Australian environment, using a variety of techniques appropriate to her design. She is currently building up a body of work for her first solo exhibition in two years' time and continues to teach around Australia.

I SAW MY FIRST QUILT in 1972 when I was living for a year with my husband and children in Hawaii, and was completely bowled over by it. It was, of course, an Hawaiian quilt.

I knew I had to make quilts but had no idea how to go about it so I bought a do-it-yourself kit for $US12.00. I followed the instructions and found, surprisingly, that I could manage the size of the thing and had the dedication necessary to finish it.

When I returned to Australia I started stitching quilts of my own imaginings. They evolved because I don't like to copy and I wanted to show things based on my own experience. Among others, I developed five quilts which I call the 'Dullflower' series. They depict native plants, and the title is a wry salute to those who find boredom in the Australian bush.

Over the years I've made many pieces, gradually increasing in design skill and confidence. I went to art school part-time for four years, not for painting and drawing as such, but as grist to the quiltmaking mill. The forty or so quilts I've made have all been different from each other and I've learnt something from each one. I've made very large and quite small quilts by hand and by machine, pieced and appliqued. I enjoy hand work best.

I didn't try to break any radical new ground with this quilt but continued to explore plant forms and expressd them through applique.

▶ **Portrait**
cottons;
hand appliqued, hand quilted

Susan Denton

❛I STILL ADMIRE OLD QUILTS BUT I NO LONGER HAVE A DESIRE TO COPY THEM❜

MELBOURNE, VIC Susan's childhood training in observation and her love of colour come together in her Seminole style work. Her concern with conservation is expressed in much of her work through carefully juxtaposed colour and considered arrangement of pieces to produce optical movement. She has been involved in exhibiting and other quilt-related projects, notably the Wool Quilt exhibition in 1985, and the book *Quiltmaking*.

I WAS BORN IN LONDON and as a child lived in various parts of England. I met my husband on a trip to Turkey and we formed the idea of travelling overland through Asia. We arrived in Australia fifteen years ago.

I did a degree when I lived in Canberra and the week I finished it I found a quiltmaking book. That's how I learnt my techniques — just from books. Like many people, I started by making traditional quilts because I didn't really think about anything else. I still admire old quilts but I no longer have a desire to copy them. I made quite a few quilts that were what I now regard as 'eastern' quilts. They were concerned with the extraordinary colours and shapes from the east.

I make quilts because of the patterns and colours and the fabrics themselves. My mother is wonderful with colour and my father, who is a scientist, was always telling me to observe things closely. We would always be peering into rock pools, finding things and looking at their various parts and shapes. This early training to be observant may have lain dormant, but now I think it has become important to my quiltmaking.

In 1983 I started playing with my recent style, connected to Seminole patchwork in its technique. This gives me a way of mixing colours — I am excited by colour and colour combinations. I made two or three quilts and then had a break at a time when I was unable to do any sewing. When I started again I found a distinct difference in my use of colour.

The first quilt I made in the Reef series was 'Oil Slick'. It's a very angry piece of work. I couldn't do any more of those quilts until I'd finished that one. It came from direct experience of an oil slick on the Great Barrier Reef which made me realise that conservation is more than hoping everything will be alright — it's got to be an active thing. The other quilts in the series are also to do with conservation, but less obviously.

'Autumn Hibiscus' is a celebration of the colours in the hibiscus bush immediately outside my workroom. It heartens me with the sunshine and shadows playing on the leaves and flowers.

▶ **Autumn Hibiscus II**
cottons, silks;
machine pieced, machine quilted

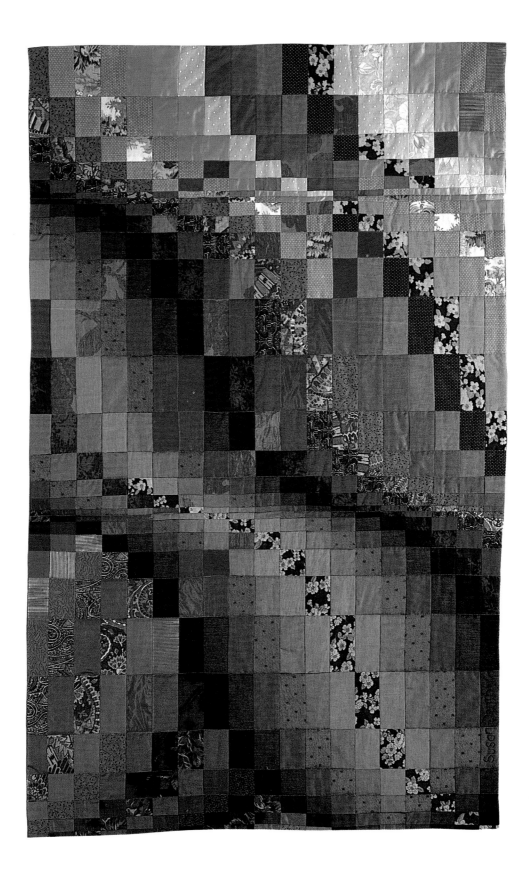

Pamela Tawton

● I LIKE TO EXPERIMENT BY
SELECTING FABRIC WITH A
PARTICULAR BLOCK OR PLAN
IN MIND, AND PLAY AROUND
WITH THE RELATIONSHIP
BETWEEN THEM ●

CANBERRA, ACT   Pamela was introduced to traditional quiltmaking while living in America and has developed her own work since returning to Australia in 1980. Although she is recognised for her skilful quilts in the stained glass style, this is only one of a variety of approaches she takes to her work. Pamela has participated in a number of local and interstate exhibitions and has conducted classes in quiltmaking for the past eight years.

M Y DEEP LOVE FOR QUILTMAKING was developed during a posting to the United States in the late 1970s. I developed initial skills by enrolling in a basic patchwork and quilting course run in conjunction with an adult education program. These skills were further honed by attending other courses and visiting exhibitions in Virginia.

Since returning to Australia I have enhanced my techniques by attending a wide range of workshops. There was a time when I would try any workshop, but now I'm more concerned to develop my own style and I've become more selective about my influences. I strive for self-improvement and to this end completed a course in fashion and design at Woden College of Technical and Further Education and a basic course in drawing.

I've been developing a style of my own based on traditional quilts with unusual colour combinations. I like to experiment by selecting fabric with a particular block or plan in mind, and play around with the relationship between them. The stained glass technique is only one of many different approaches I've experimented with. I have produced many quilts in my own right and in conjunction with others, participating in a number of friendship quilts. I've taught quiltmaking for the last eight years. I derive a great deal of satisfaction in sharing my skills with the many students who attend my classes.

My most successful quilt, to date, is certainly 'Flora Australiana' (featured in *Australian Patchwork* by Margaret Rolfe) and another quilt, 'Clairvoyance', received a judge's commendation.

▶ **Morning Call**
cottons, polycottons, furnishing fabrics;
hand stitched, machine edged, hand quilted

Suzanne Dowsett

● I'M MORE INTERESTED IN

TRADITIONAL PATTERN AND

STYLE THAN IN THE ART

QUILT ●

PERTH, WA   In stepping outside her usual traditional approach and designing a quilt specific to an idea, Suzanne shows her adaptability. Nevertheless, her interest remains with tradition. She began quilting about six years ago. She is a member of the Western Australian Quilters' Association and has served as secretary and artistic director of the '84 Quilt Show, and co-ordinator of the National Trust Quilt Project. Suzanne is a cartographer, a profession which obviously influenced the design of 'Southland'.

I MIGRATED TO AUSTRALIA from the cotton-farming area of Mississippi twenty-two years ago. My family was originally of Pennsylvania Dutch origin. My great-grandmother was a quilter who made 183 quilts and documented them all. My mother and I are attempting to trace as many as we can. We know of thirteen and every so often a relative or friend of a friend turns one up.

I once went to a quilt show with a friend, and I couldn't get out of there quickly enough to try my hand at it. Then, as I became interested, I started having flashbacks. I remember the best quilts that came out only for company on the beds. When I was a child I remember helping Mamaw cut up pieces that were eventually made into a quilt for her by her mother.

Now quilting is *the* over-riding interest in my life. I live in a home unit, so I don't have a big work space — I've never had anywhere big enough to leave things out. That's what's so good about fabrics: you can put them away.

I'm more interested in traditional pattern and style than in the art quilt. It takes a little time to develop, but because I like country furnishings and country quilts I'll always be interested in the traditional. I suppose the map quilt is the furthest I've ever diverged from the block style, but there I'm still using something that already existed: the map itself.

For the suitcase exhibition I wanted something that was Australian and particularly West Australian. I therefore used the mariner's compass from the map of De Vlamingh's voyage in 1697. Superimposed over the grid is the coastline of Western Australia (also from De Vlamingh's chart) from the Swan River in the south to the Northwest Cape. The ribbon highlights the Dutch name for Australia, *tZuydlandt* or 'Southland'. The fabrics were chosen to call to mind the colours of an antique map. The Australian green and gold were muted to the grey-green of the bush and the beige of the landscape. The feathery Liberty print reminded me of seaweed and underwater plants, and the wool batt refers to the time when our country 'rode on the sheep's back'.

▶ Southland
polished cotton, cotton, Liberty lawn, calico;
hand and machine piecing, applique, hand quilting

A n n L h u e d e

●I AM FASCINATED BY THE
LIMITLESS SCOPE OF THIS
CRAFT. IT HAS ENABLED
ME . . . TO PUT MY ARTISTIC
ENDEAVOUR INTO
QUILTS . . . ●

MELBOURNE, VIC   Ann came to
quiltmaking after a full career in
nursing and found it to be a
personally expressive medium. She
enjoys experimenting with colour
and block designs.

I TRAINED AS A NURSE IN PERTH, and in 1964 married and had five
children in quick succession. I wasn't a sewer or a designer; I was
a theatre nurse for twenty-nine of my nursing years and not much else.

Until 1980 my needlework was limited to normal family needs. I
came into quiltmaking fairly late but it has developed into an engross-
ing interest over the last eight years. Initially I followed traditional
designs, but gradually drifted into making my own designs and experimenting with colour. Even now I'm learning new things. I am fascinated by the limitless scope of this craft. It has enabled me, as a rank
amateur, to put my artistic endeavour into quilts, whereas I couldn't
on paper.

I was born in Wiluna in the desert of Western Australia. During
the war years we lived in the south-west of the state. On rare occasions
there you can see the Aurora Australis in the sky. I have vague memories of being taken out of bed one night to see these colours. It was
like a sunset with lots of yellows, but covering the sky. I made this
quilt from a sketch I had worked on in a design class and I've named
it after those southern lights.

▶ **Southern Lights**
cottons;
hand pieced, hand quilted

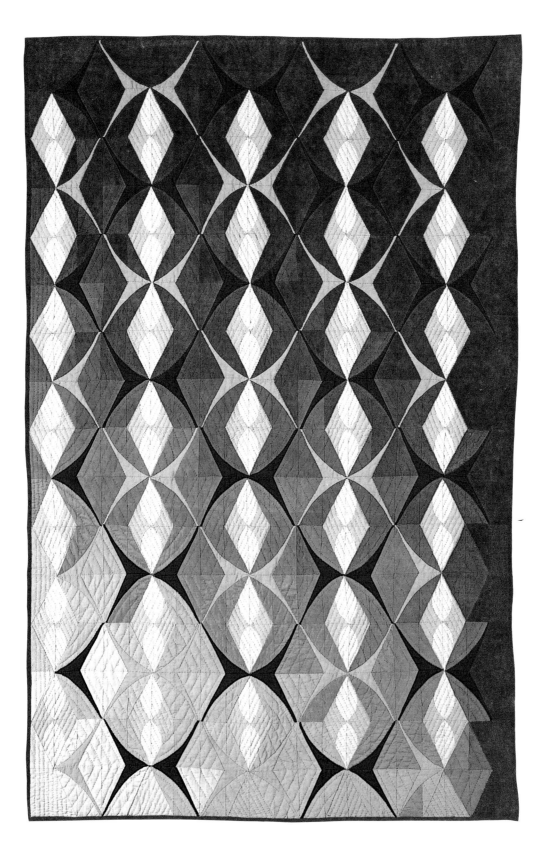

Penelope Whitchurch

●I HAVE ALWAYS BEEN
ENGAGED IN TESTING EACH
TECHNIQUE FOR ITS
POSSIBILITIES AND
RESTRICTIONS●

PERTH, WA   Penelope has been
engaged in textiles since the sixties,
first as instructor at Technical
College and later as lecturer at the
West Australian Institute of
Technology (now Curtin
University). Among other textile
skills, she teaches the Dispersol dye
technique which she uses in her
own work. Penelope has devised a
means of creating patchwork
effects by piecing dye-on-paper
designs and transferring them to
whole cloth. This she enhances
with stitched and beaded effects.

Mᴀ INTEREST IN QUILTING started seriously with an Australia-wide
quilting competition in 1976. I decided to participate to avoid
the prospect of judging the competition. I worked the traditional hexagon within organic shapes like seedpods, and heavily embroidered
them on calico, quilting it with backstitch. I won the first prize and
have been smitten ever since.

As a lecturer I feel it is important to become acquainted with each
new technique that becomes available and I have always been engaged
in testing each technique for its possibilities and restrictions. I use the
Dispersol dye technique in my own quilts. I draw a lot, so it's natural
for me to use a brush and pen and ink. I draw with the dye on to
paper and heat transfer this image to the polyester fabric.

For 'Zagarat II' I cut up some of the design sheets I use for
demonstrating the technique and reassembled them to my design. I
then used them as iron-on transfers, printing on to the fabric. I followed this with quilting and embroidery with beading.

The severe quality of line in this quilt is reminiscent of eighth
century Assyria. Buildings at that time were severe of line and even
headgear had a rectangular quality, fitting solidly on massive head and
hair. The top centre of the quilt holds 'building blocks' tumbling down
into a woven shape standing on horizontal beams and upright pillars.
The diagonal shapes at the top of the quilt branch sharply skyward like
wings in flight. Light, cloudlike colours are used for a dreamy effect.

▶ **Zagarat II**
polyester, beads, pure silk thread;
Dispersol dye technique, hand
embroidered, beaded and quilted

Jane Long

● 'COSMOS' IS AN EXERCISE IN
FORM, COLOUR AND
TEXTURE. I LIKE SIMPLE
SHAPES AND THE
INTERACTION OF COLOUR ●

MELBOURNE, VIC Jane's sense
of design is expressed through her
quiltmaking. Since studying textile
design three years ago, she has
evolved simple forms and
complementary colours in her
work. She has exhibited in several
quilt exhibitions.

I'VE ALWAYS LOVED QUILTS since I slept under one at my grand-mother's house at a very early age. It was made of black cotton satin and mattress ticking, lined with red flannel.

The first quilt I made was for my son nineteen years ago, but I had too many family commitments to concentrate on patchwork until the mid-eighties, when I studied textile design at Warrnambool College of Technical and Further Education. My lecturer, Marie Cook, was a tremendous help in developing my ability to design my own quilts.

I have used the applique technique but I prefer piecing quilts. I've made some traditional quilts for beds, but wall pieces are designed specifically.

Paul Klee's work has been an indirect influence in my work. His use of squares and lines with muted and graded colours appeal to me.

'Cosmos' is an exercise in form, colour and texture. I like simple shapes and the interaction of colour. The values of red, neutral brown and black combine with one dark shade of green. This khaki, with its complement of red, makes all the browns in the quilt appear to be green. A member of my quilting group suggested the name because of the circles, and I thought it was appropriate.

▶ **Cosmos**
cottons;
machine pieced, hand
appliqued and quilted

Christa Roksandic

❝THERE'S NO OTHER CRAFT WHERE I CAN EXPRESS MYSELF AS I CAN WITH QUILTS BECAUSE I CAN MAKE A THING AND SAY SOMETHING WITH IT AS WELL❞

CANBERRA, ACT Since beginning to make quilts in 1984 Christa has evolved her own distinctive design style. She takes her imagery from the natural environment and translates it through a curved piecing technique she derived from the traditional Drunkard's Path block. Her family commitments are met by disciplining her quiltmaking to regular working hours in a studio nearby.

AFTER MANY YEARS AS A NEEDLEPOINTER, cross-stitcher and lead-lighter, I made a move into quiltmaking about four years ago. Once I started I knew 'that was it'; I wanted to stay with it as a commitment. It took over my life. I used to quilt until two o'clock in the morning and couldn't seem to stop myself. I felt that quiltmaking had chosen me and I couldn't change it.

I didn't do traditional work at all. I kept seeing much greater possibilities in designing whole quilts from the original blocks. I became totally absorbed in a technique using almost entirely curved piecing which I found useful in my landscape designs. In 1986–87 I completed a quilt called 'Living Together'. This quilt was my first effort in exploring the sea and I had great pleasure in creating a series of 'water' quilts.

I had to make a conscious effort to curb my enthusiasm in order to catch up with all the responsibilities a young family brings. I'm now working from nine till three in a studio away from home because I couldn't bear to see all the things around me that I should have been doing instead of quilting. The workshops I attended given by interstate and overseas artists were precious to me. I felt a strengthening of my desire to learn more and develop my skills further.

I've been looking for a better way of working with my pieced landscapes and I have one project which is different from my previous work. I am experimenting with silk painting, planning to blend pieces in with others. There's no other craft where I can express myself as I can with quilts because I can make a thing and say something with it as well.

▶ **Pretty Point Bay**
cottons, cotton blends, silks;
machine pieced, hand quilted

Jenni Albanis

❛I WORK WITHIN THE
FRAMEWORK OF THE
TRADITIONAL BLOCK BUT
GIVE IT MY OWN LOOK, AND
I LIKE TO USE A GREAT MANY
DIFFERENT FABRICS❜

MELBOURNE, VIC The
ambience in Jenni's home supports
her quiltmaking. Her family all
want quilts and enjoy seeing them
hanging in the house. She is on the
committee of the Australian
Quilters' Association and has a
small group that meets in her
home. Jenni is currently working
on a quilt that expresses the
meaning of winter for her.

WE'VE BEEN BASED IN ESSENDON since we were married and live
in an old suburban house on a fairly large block of land. I enjoy
gardening and was inspired to make my quilt because I love the riot
of colour that autumn in Melbourne brings. I have a golden ash at the
front of my house and there are many liquidambers and other autumn-
colouring trees in the street beyond.

Looking around, there are enough quilts in my home to show it's
a quilter's house. My family is proud of it — they don't resent my
time spent quilting. I don't want to sell quilts — I'd rather keep them
or give them away. I've given two to a niece who keeps having babies.

I was interested in dolls' clothes, and did needlework at school. I
still have a little cloth embroidered with tiny chickens that I made
when I was a student. My mother was a dressmaker and was a big
influence on my life until I came to quilting. Then I was out into a
field that none of my family had ever been involved with.

I work within the framework of the traditional block but give it my
own look, and I like to use a great many different fabrics. I have a
great love of colour, and quilts *are* colour — at least, mine are. I want
to work with colour shading in traditional blocks. The shading will
colour over the edge of the block so that I get an overall shading that
diminishes the effect of the original block.

I find quilting soothing and enjoy creating lovely things. It's interesting but it's more than that — it's a passion. I couldn't give it up if
I tried. If I had known how much it would take over my life, I would
have been frightened!

▶ **Autumn**
cottons;
hand pieced, hand quilted

Muriel Floyd

●I FELT I WANTED TO SHOW
SOMETHING OF EACH STATE
AND OF THE COUNTRY AS A
WHOLE . . .●

SYDNEY, NSW Muriel's quilt
features a garland of native
Australian flowers in the centre of
a softly quilted background. The
flowers are emblems of the
individual Australian states and the
nation. She has worked these
motifs in shadow applique, an
intricate technique she often uses
in her quilts.

THE UNUSUAL COLOURS AND FORMS of Australian wildflowers are
appealing and are used as symbols on many articles in everyday
use. For this small quilt I felt I wanted to show something of each state
and of the country as a whole, so I went to the library and read about
the national and state emblems and designed a garland of them. I
showed the native heath for Victoria, the Cooktown orchid for
Queensland, Mangle's kangaroo paw for Western Australia and Sturt's
desert pea for South Australia. The Northern Territory uses Sturt's
desert rose, which is quite different although similar in name to the
desert pea. Tasmania has the blue gum, New South Wales the
waratah, the Australian Capital Territory has the royal bluebell and,
of course, the national emblem is the green and gold of the wattle.

Converting my design on paper to expression in fabric was a challenge. I shadow appliqued the flower shapes on to the background and
quilted around them. To do the shadow work I cut out each little
shape in the coloured fabric, covered it with the same shape in organza,
which softened the whole effect, and stitched it in place on the quilt.

For the past ten years quilts have been my greatest interest. When
I visited the United States in 1982 this interest was further stimulated
through observations and workshops. I usually make pieced quilts but
the shadow applique took my eye some years ago and I've done quite
a few of them. It's quite slow but I enjoy it.

► **Floral Emblems**
cottons, organza;
shadow applique, hand quilted

Beryl Hodges

●ALTHOUGH YOU ARE IN TOTAL CONTROL OF THE MEDIUM, WONDERFUL SURPRISES CAN APPEAR FROM THE COMBINATIONS OF FABRICS●

PERTH, WA   From a long background in needlework, Beryl began quilting in 1980. She experiments with variations of strip piecing, using vibrant colour combinations. Although she moves house almost every two years, she has been involved with organisations and teaching quiltmaking where possible.

As long as I can remember I've sewed and enjoyed some form of needlework. In the late 1970s I was living in Sydney and saw an exhibition of Canadian quilts at the Rocks. It was a time when quilts were becoming exposed here in Australia. I heard there were quilting classes being held in Mosman but we were living out towards Parramatta and it was physically impossible for me to get to them. Later we moved to Canberra and I discovered the Patchwork Group (now Canberra Quilters) and began to learn.

Once I started, I couldn't stop. There's something special about quiltmaking. It seems to attune to your personality and become absorbed into it. Although you are in total control of the medium, wonderful surprises can appear from the combinations of fabrics. I love to handle fabric, to fold and rearrange it, to absorb colour and effect by feeling and working with it.

I enjoy experimenting with the log cabin style, testing and plying it in different formations. In 'Celebration Sky' I've used a triangular log cabin, which is something I hadn't tried before. I wanted to convey a sense of fireworks — half-star, half-explosion.

When selecting for my quilts, I'm not as concerned about the fabric composition as with its colour. I look for 'zingy' colours. I love the effect of black in intensifying colours and making them glow.

I make quilts for my own satisfaction. I've only been able to give away one quilt as a gift. I feel much too connected to them. We move quite often. My husband is in the Army and this is our seventeenth home. At different times I've taken over the whole house with fabrics and sewing machine — Army houses are not built with artists' studios.

I'm a school teacher by profession. I've lost touch with whether it's natural for me to teach or if it's a learned skill. Either way, I love this contact with others and enjoy seeing people who couldn't thread a needle or who had never quilted before feel they've gained something. It fascinates me that quilting puts creativity within reach of anyone by offering varying levels of achievement. Trying a traditional pattern allows choice of colour, pattern and inter-relation, while at the other end of the spectrum you can be totally unconventional.

▶ **Celebration Sky**
cottons, polycottons;
machine pieced, machine and
hand quilted

Hilda Farquhar-Smith

❝I LIKE THE RICHNESS OF EMBELLISHMENT YOU CAN GET FROM USING DIFFERENT THREADS. TEXTILES ARE FASCINATING BECAUSE THEY ARE MORE THREE DIMENSIONAL THAN PAINTING❞

SYDNEY, NSW   After a career in advertising, Hilda became interested in embroidery when a friend suggested she attend a creative class. Her involvement with the Embroiderers' Guild began in 1972 and she has been both president and vice-president over the past five years. She translates her graphic art influence into her quilts with the use of flowing forms and complementary quilting concepts.

I HAD FOUR YEARS AT SWINBURNE. I did the certificate of art for two years and then concentrated on advertising (they call it graphic arts now) for my diploma. I spent the best part of ten years working in the studio of one of the larger advertising agencies in Melbourne, where I was involved with magazine and daily press work.

After I was married and came to New South Wales, I noticed that Hannah Frew was tutoring for the Embroiderers' Guild. She had a free and vibrant style in her use of stitching and colour. I thought that one day that would be for me but I was living in the country at that stage. It wasn't until we came to Sydney that I was able to join the Embroiderers' Guild. I'd joined a friend's tennis group and one of the girls there had brought her patchwork and was working on it at the tennis. She was going along to a class of creative embroidery and invited me to go with her. So that was my introduction to the Embroiderers' Guild, really.

I like quilting because you can join up large areas of colour quickly, whereas if you're embroidering you might be stitching for nights to fill the same area. I like the richness of embellishment you can get from using different threads. Textiles are fascinating because they are more three dimensional than painting. I enjoy stitching the pieces and quilting but I prefer the quilt line to have something to say or to complement the piecing. I think it's much more satisfying if the quilting is integral to the original concept.

I like flowing lines and have been working with them since I started quilting. 'Square Three' started with a pieced tablecloth I made for a guild exhibition where I used a streamer motif. I enjoyed the effect and have continued with it. I am particularly interested in getting away from the angular concept of many quilts and enjoy working with curves and a feeling of movement. My last quilt was a change, based on squares, and with 'Square Three' I was still thinking about squares and the flowing shapes became superimposed over them.

▶ **Square Three**
cottons, polycottons;
machine pieced and hand quilted

Lois Densham

● MY QUILTS ARE OFTEN
MADE FROM 'OP-SHOP'
FABRICS BUT THEY'RE
ALWAYS THINGS THAT
REMIND ME OF PEOPLE ●

MELBOURNE, VIC Lois has recently been working as artist/resource person in two country communities and as an artist-in-school in Melbourne. Teaching is fulfilling work for her; although she likes to be alone at times, she enjoys 'going out the front door and meeting people'.

I REALLY STARTED ON TEXTILES in the seventies. I'd done jewellery, lampshades, anything before that. It's a family tradition; we weren't sporty, we used to make things. My independence is important and I live alone, but I have a close relationship with my sisters and their children as part of an extended family, which gives a strong sense of belonging.

My work has changed as it's gone along. At one stage, it used to be landscape-like but I feel now that I've gone from that through other stages. I'm trying to get people to look at all these surfaces. I think I'm experimenting in how to get people to really look into a piece of work.

I can become quite involved with little bits of material. My quilts are often made from 'op-shop' fabrics but they're always things that remind me of people. The hankies I use are those people have given me so, to me, they represent the people themselves. When people see these things in my work, they are reminded of their own life and their own associations. That goes for people I don't know as well, because they can make their own connections.

I've just worked with a group of Kampuchean children. There were twenty kids (mostly boys) making about sixty quilts. They just kept working! One girl was inspired by a traditional quilt one of the teachers had brought in, and she got some fabric, went chop, chop and made it up in two weeks. It lacks fine stitching quality but she's very pleased — she has it on her bed now.

I looked after a bird once. It had a beautiful cage but the door was always open. 'Birds in a Gilded Cage' is about not being confined to a cage, even though it may be beautiful, but being outside and free.

▶ **Birds in a Gilded Cage**
cotton hankies, calico, tweed, braid, beads and buttons; stencils, silk screening, painting, machine applique, hand embroidery

Helen Macartney

❝I WAS INSPIRED BY THE COLOURS IN THIS PART OF THE COUNTRY WHERE THE LAND DOMINATES AND OVERWHELMS HUMAN SETTLEMENT❞

SYDNEY, NSW   Helen's career was in teaching English and History when her travels to Europe, India and Asia stimulated her interest in textiles and art. Since her postgraduate Diploma in Professional Art Studies at Alexander Mackie (Sydney, 1980) she has worked as a textile artist, teaching English to adult migrants part-time. She participated in Craft Expo '85 and has exhibited in various quilt exhibitions since 1981.

AT SCHOOL I HAD a very verbal orientation. I was interested in colour and texture, but this was muted. Mum always made our clothes when we were young, and then my sister and I made our own, but it was travelling in Europe and Asia that sparked something off. I saw an exhibition of old Canadian quilts in London and they were wonderful! I began making quilts while I was travelling and kept on making small quilts for recreation.

I didn't have any 'proper' art training but friends encouraged me to see that as a freedom, rather than a lack. I used to try sketching things out but it was no good. I just have to go straight into it, and let the subconscious come through so that whatever intuitive and spontaneous creativity I have is allowed to function without the conscious mind censoring it.

My postgraduate course at Alexander Mackie was a good stimulus. It was a case of 'do your own thing and bring it in to be commented on'. That helped my confidence because I had a very positive response.

My major recreation with my husband is to walk in the bush. There's a wholeness there — everything is in harmony. It's a restorative thing, too.

When I made this quilt I had just returned from a month's trip to Alice Springs and the centre of Australia. I was inspired by the colours in this part of the country where the land dominates and overwhelms human settlement. The patterns, lines and colours in the fabrics are all very much of the earth and growing things, and the ambience of the 'Red Centre' was, undoubtedly, a strong influence. That visit to central Australia just fired me. I'd like to go back there for a few weeks every year.

▶ **Earth Rhythms**
screen printed cottons, batik
(both bought and self-made),
Italian silk;
machine pieced and hand quilted

Alison Muir

❝THE STRUCTURE IS VERY
IMPORTANT. EVERYTHING
HAS AN INHERENT
STRUCTURE AND MY
TRAINING IS TO RECOGNISE
THAT AND WORK WITH IT❞

SYDNEY, NSW The intense colours of Amish quilts aroused Alison's interest when she saw them exhibited in Ohio (USA) in 1982. Alison's career as an interior designer runs hand-in-hand with her approach to making quilts. She often works with several at one time. Alison sometimes accepts commissions and shows her work through quilt exhibitions.

THE FACT THAT I COULD FORM a structure and repeat it appealed to me. I felt comfortable making the structure in fabrics because I'd always made my own clothes. As an interior designer I had a range of fabric samples to choose from — often co-ordinated or the same fabric in different colours — so I developed designs with graduating effects.

Making quilts plays a very important part in my life. Professionally, the more I get into management, the less I design. Making a quilt involves the same designing process as designing an office or hotel; there's the image in your mind's eye, you develop that image and document it so that someone else can build it. But with quilts, I build it myself.

Design is my first consideration, then selecting fabrics to portray it. I often use natural elements as a theme, as in 'Southerly' and 'Dust Storm'. I've always lived by the water and 'Sand Dune' relates to that.

The structure is very important. Everything has an inherent structure and my training is to recognise that and work with it. In other quilts I've always designed the blocks myself. 'Sand Dune' was the first quilt in which I used traditonal blocks and I've pushed the forms to use them in a different way.

▶ **Sand Dune**
cotton, polycotton, silk, polyester;
hand pieced, hand appliqued,
machine quilted

Rose Marie Szulc

ABORIGINES ARE PROBABLY the most disadvantaged group in the Australian community, yet they have a much longer history here than any other settlers. We must have proper respect for their culture, their ownership of the land and their 'shining pure spirit'.

The Aborigines' struggle is our struggle — we must not forget. We must recognise the status of Aborigines.

They deserve a future too!

●THE ABORIGINES'
STRUGGLE IS OUR STRUGGLE
— WE MUST NOT FORGET.
WE MUST RECOGNISE THE
STATUS OF ABORIGINES●

MELBOURNE, VIC   Rose Marie has made her quilt to represent her support for the Aboriginal people of Australia. She chooses to remind us of the Aboriginal cause for cultural dignity in their own land.

▶ **Memory Piece II**
corduroy, gaberdine, cotton knit, net, prints, buttons, kilt pins, diamantes, copper trim, cotton thread; backing: 'Steelwool Island' print on cotton voile; hand and machine sewn

Leslye O'Sullivan

❝I HAVE A GOOD SENSE OF COLOUR. THIS IS MY STARTING POINT IN DESIGNING AND IT SUGGESTS THE DIRECTION OF THE REST OF THE QUILT❞

HAZELBROOK, NSW Leslye first touched on quiltmaking during her training as a designer in the fashion industry. Later she expanded this initial interest, applying her six years of experience in the trade, and has been able to combine creative satisfaction and productivity.

IN 1975 I DID A FASHION CERTIFICATE COURSE which touched on patchwork quiltmaking and candlewicking. I was very interested then but was eager to get out into the trade. For six years I worked as a designer in the fashion industry, first in Sydney and then, after I married, in Melbourne. When my daughter was born I started my own business from home, manufacturing clothing. Several of these garments featured piecing and applique, an interest I'd felt earlier.

After my marriage I moved back to Sydney with my daughter and, with the need to be self-sufficient, took to making patchwork quilts. It was another avenue for design and I found it was both creative and productive. Initially I made bedspreads but I'm starting to make wall-hangings and personalised commissions. I use applique on the garments and piecing for the wall-hangings and commissions.

I have a good sense of colour. This is my starting point in designing and it suggests the direction of the rest of the quilt. I like quilts to have movement and flow. I tend to incorporate the same thing in the garments I design, creating movement around the body shape.

I piece and quilt by machine because it is the only way I can keep my hands up with my ideas. I reworked my 'Flying Geese' quilt several times until I was happy with it. The original design was very different from the finished piece. I began using pastel colours but when I changed to more vibrant shades, the shapes began to do what I wanted.

I've been living in the Blue Mountains for the past four years. The people here are generally involved and aware of art and craft and this provides an encouraging environment for me. I feel that I can express myself more individually than I've been able to through the limitations of the fashion industry. I plan to go back to Technical College next year to expand my teaching qualifications so that I can teach fashion design at a tertiary level.

▶ **Flying Geese**
cottons, polycottons;
machine pieced, machine quilted

Narelle Grieve

●QUILTERS ARE SPECIAL
PEOPLE, I THINK; THEY'RE
SHARING PEOPLE●

SYDNEY, NSW   When Narelle took up quilting as an interest she discovered more than a pastime. She found companionship and an addictive enthusiasm for making quilts which she passes on to others through her teaching and public talks. She acquired her teaching qualifications in America and feels strongly that her workshops should give participants sound knowledge and satisfaction. The same pride of achievement is important to her in making her own quilts.

WE MOVED TO PENNSYLVANIA in December 1981 and stayed four and a half years. Our furniture took three months longer than we did to get there. I'm a person who can't sit still very long — I've got to be doing something — so I started going to quilting classes. We lived about a half-hour drive from Lancaster County where the Amish quilters are. I especially love the antique Amish quilts and think the use of black in some of them is wonderful. The first thing I did was an Amish-style quilt.

While I was in America I went to as many workshops as I could. I fiddled around with traditional patterns and came up with my own arrangement. I still like traditional quilts more than contemporary ones.

I like the subtle whole cloth look — it's my very favourite style of quilt. I've got three daughters and I'm making a quilt for each of them. I've made one already and the second one is on the frame now. I especially like white on white and, with the one I'm doing now, I'm using a silk thread. It pulls through so easily.

I have a small collection of antique quilts and visit charity organisations and interested groups to give talks about them. I want to encourage people to think about quilts. Quite often they'll trigger off someone's memory — they're living history. I introduced my mother to quilting about seven years ago: she's made about ten quilts since then. She's amazing!

When I designed 'Wattle and Daub' I was trying to think of something I could use that was Australian but wasn't wildflowers and animals. I love old houses, and the colonial slab huts go right back to the beginning of our history. I wanted to involve people in the quilt somehow, and showing their homes suggested something of how they lived. I took the pictures from Daphne Kingston's book *Old Slab Houses of Early Sydney* (with permission) and embroidered them in backstitch. I used flowers in trapunto on the border.

▶ **Wattle and Daub**
calico;
backstitch embroidery, hand quilted and trapunto

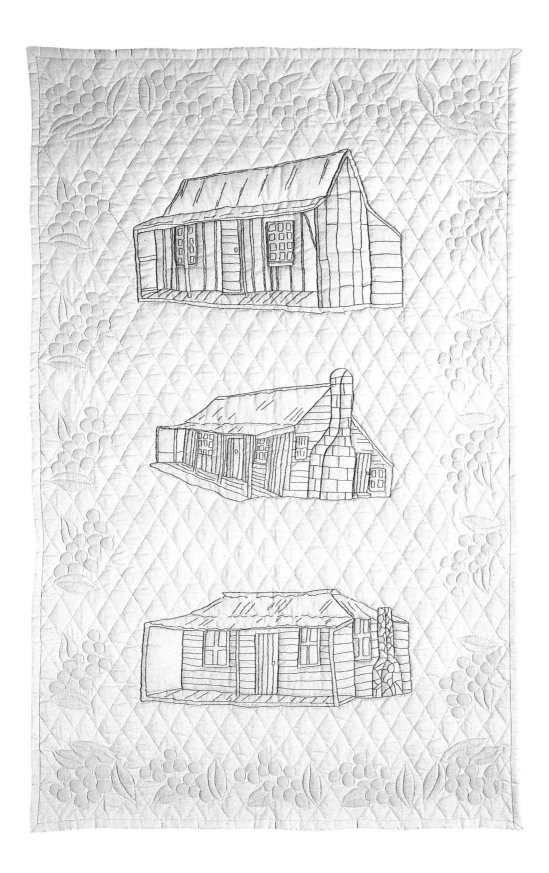

Denise Vanderlugt

●THE COLOURS ARE THOSE OF TROPICAL NORTH QUEENSLAND WHERE EVERYTHING SEEMS LARGER AND MORE EXTREME THAN IN OTHER PLACES●

PROSERPINE, QLD Denise expresses her love of nature and colour and her tropical surroundings through the medium of hand quilting and applique. She produces her work as an individual expression, sometimes to commission, and exhibits with her husband, who is a sculptor.

I LIVE ON FIVE ACRES of rainforest that I'm regenerating and clearing of lantana. I'm surrounded by the clear atmosphere of the Whitsundays. The cool aquas and blues, the rich greens and exotic colours are all around me and it's hard not to put them into my work.

I remember that as a little girl, if I had any spare time, I'd be 'mucking up' bits of material and embroidering them. Now I enjoy doing it with my own fabrics. I was introduced to quilting when I was supervisor of a craft program in an old people's home in Canada. Six years ago I gave up working at the Handicap Centre in Proserpine to begin full-time quilting.

In 'My Garden' I have food plants to attract the exotic Ulysses and Cairns birdwing butterflies, nectar-bearing flowers to attract noisy rainbow lorikeets and tiny sunbirds, and seeds falling to the ground from fruit-bearing rainforest trees to feed the lovely green-winged pigeon. All these creatures visit my garden and have provided inspiration for this quilt. The colours are those of tropical North Queensland where everything seems larger and more extreme than in other places.

▶ **My Garden**
cotton, polycotton, stranded embroidery thread;
hand appliqued, hand quilted and embroidered

"My Garden"   Renee Vanderbilt © 1987

Rachel Dettman

❝I PREFER A QUILT TO TAKE ME A LONG TIME SO THAT I CAN DEVELOP A RELATIONSHIP WITH IT❞

ADELAIDE, SA When Rachel came to Australia from Indiana, USA, she felt she was quilting in isolation. Participation in the Quantum Leaps Quilt Show was her first opportunity to see other people's work and to find the enthusiasm that comes through a shared interest. In addition to her work as Special Education Adviser to Catholic Education, Rachel has been actively involved in quilting initiatives; notably, the forming of The Quilters' Guild of South Australia and 'Quilted Visions', a collaborative project between quilters and artists.

QUILTS HAVE ALWAYS BEEN PART OF MY LIFE from the times I visited my grandmother's house in Georgia, USA, and saw quilts on the beds and stacked in the cupboards, or visited museums when I was growing up. I'm attracted to things with a sense of history.

My older sister has a real sense of history too, and it was she who suggested I make a quilt for the American bicentennial celebrations. Neither of us had ever done such a thing in our lives but I thought, well why *not* make a quilt?

My husband challenged me that I would never finish it and that was enough — I finished it in ten months. After that I was hooked.

My lack of formal art training allows me to think more in terms of folk art. I'm attracted to this style because it's fresh, simple and unpretentious but hopefully can reveal flashes of inspiration through the creative use of the medium. It's as if quilt art inspires an innate sense of form and design.

I think of myself as an old-fashioned patchworker and quilter who cannot be rushed. The rest of my life is very busy and I want to keep my creative work at a gentle pace so that I can be more reflective with the making of each quilt. There is a sort of rhythm that comes from sewing tiny stitch after tiny stitch. It provides me with time to unwind, meditate and create. I enjoy working with small pieces and printed fabrics. I prefer a quilt to take me a long time so that I can develop a relationship with it.

In these days of mass-produced items, I join with other women who like to make their surroundings and possessions uniquely their own. My quilts hang on the walls of my home and cover our beds and we like being surrounded by them. My goal is simply to make a dozen or more major pieces in my lifetime to pass on as heirlooms.

I chose the star pattern for this quilt because I wanted to play with a border and linear print in the centre sections. There was no preconceived colour design; only the selection of compatible fabrics for the centre designs to radiate just as a kaleidoscope changes. Each star seemed to make itself as, eventually, did the rest of the quilt.

▶ **Blue Kaleidoscope**
plain and patterned cottons;
hand pieced and hand quilted

Robyn Kinsela

I AM METICULOUS AND ORDERED IN MY APPROACH. THE FABRIC COLLAGE USES THESE QUALITIES AND ALLOWS A FLEXIBILITY TO REARRANGE AS THE WORK DEVELOPS

MITTAGONG, NSW Robyn's earlier career in the design field has overtaken her interest in quilts, giving way to a more graphic approach. She is more concerned with achieving a visual result than in traditional techniques, which has led her to develop her fabric collage.

I've always been interested in painting and drawing, fine art and colour and design. At first I went into the design field to make a secure living rather than face the uncertainty of an artist's income. What I've eventually done is marry all the things I like doing in fabric collage.

An important time for me was when I stopped working to have children. I found I had much more creative energy and began giving quilting classes. I understood the basis of colour and design and learnt the techniques of patchwork as I went.

To get to the end of the process in my own quilts was tedious. I was frustrated by the time-consuming traditions of quiltmaking, so I began to make fabric collage wall pieces. The soft tactile quality of traditional quilts had to be sacrificed for precision, flatness and rigidity to achieve the visual result much more quickly. I'm not a purist, so glue has replaced stitches. I am meticulous and ordered in my approach. The fabric collage uses these qualities and allows a flexibility to rearrange as the work develops.

I branched away from quilting by making a range of greeting cards in collage. When I was accepted into Craft Expo '86 with a few initial wall pieces I had six months to formulate bigger works. The exposure there attracted commissions from a number of architects and developers, which is where I get most of my work now. My design background and organisation help me here. I can be given a direction and work to it, and the discipline of my natural working style is an advantage.

▶ **Wriggle**
cottons, polycottons, synthetics, towelling inner;
heat-sensitive glued fabrics in jigsaw formation, machine pieced

Margot Child

●MY QUILTS ARE BASED ON
SIMPLE, UNIVERSAL
PATTERNS AND I REGARD
THEM AS PART OF A FOLK
ART TRADITION . . .●

SYDNEY, NSW   Margot's family tradition was in embroidery and dressmaking and she has maintained this through her own life. After graduating in Science, she worked as a dietitian (among other things) and has always enjoyed sewing as a private interest. She began making quilts in 1981 and joined the Quilters' Guild at its first meeting. She has exhibited in Guild and regional exhibitions and although she's sold a few quilts, she's 'mostly given them away'.

MY MOTHER TAUGHT ME TO SEW — both practical things like clothes and curtains for everyday use and 'fancywork' for pleasure. And of course I grew up in a time when needlework was strong in schools and every girl was expected to know how to sew. I went from high school to university — a big thing for a sixteen-year-old. There were not many women in Science in those days and I found myself in a suddenly expanded world.

Then came work, marriage, three daughters and a busy life with the usual things. I've benefited enormously from daughters who have studied art and I did have a huge collection of scraps from making children's clothes!

I've always liked order out of disorder. I like mosaics, crystals in chemistry, that sort of thing. That's really where my interest in quilt design began. Fabric is very evocative for me. I can conjure up memories of the texture and pattern of certain materials in my past. And sewing has always been one of the things I have chosen to do with my spare time. It's balm to the soul.

In 1977 I went to New York and in a very classy shop window saw an antique Star of Bethlehem quilt. I stood there at night and drew it up. I still have it in my notebook. When I saw an exhibition in Sydney in 1981, I quickly made a connection between that Star of Bethlehem and the contemporary work on show there. It had a vitality that attracted me and I've been hooked ever since.

I don't attempt art quilts; I like the 'old quilt' thing. My quilts are based on simple, universal patterns and I regard them as part of a folk art tradition, made to use on beds.

Having always lived in Sydney, I chose the Royal Easter Show as my subject because it is the folk festival I know best. The pinwheels on sticks that children carry at the show are there as a foreground and I've tried to evoke the fun and colour of farm produce and animals, flowers, fancywork, fireworks and so on.

▶ **The Show**
printed and plain fabrics;
hand pieced, hand quilted

Deborah Brearley

●THE IMAGERY I USE IS
FROM INSPIRATION. IT
REFLECTS MY LIFE MORE
THAN IT EXPRESSES MY
EMOTIONS, EVEN THOUGH
I'M EMOTIONALLY
MOTIVATED●

QUEENSCLIFF, VIC   Originally a
ceramist, Deborah has consciously
chosen to transfer her creative
medium to textiles. As well as her
own enjoyment of the medium
and the synthesis of techniques in
her work, Deborah has extended
herself to teaching, writing books
and adaptation to commercial
enterprise. Her natural
environment is very important to
her and is a constant source of
reflection and inspiration.

I LOVE MY GARDEN AND NATURE and I'm inspired by the things around me. I love observing and watching closely — it's the subtle things that hold the most beauty. I'm a conservationist and I think there's much to learn if we look around.

I come from a ceramics background but textile suits my lifestyle now. It's portable, clean and immediate and, with a young family, I can set up amongst everything and still be creative.

I've had nine years of teaching in secondary schools and five years at district branches of the Council of Adult Education. We do patchwork and applique, fabric dyeing, painting and stencilling. I enjoy being able to transfer a message to someone — to overcome their reluctance and to exchange information and see them enjoy it. As well as that, I get out of home and interact with others. I regularly go to short courses offered at the Meat Market craft centre. These have included screen printing, commercial repeat systems, photographic screen processes and feltmaking.

Quilting puts together a lot of things I like doing: painting, dyeing, hand stitching, machine stitching, printing. The imagery I use is from inspiration. It reflects my life more than it expresses my emotions, even though I'm emotionally motivated.

'Fragility' symbolises the cycle of life. The earth and sky, the female and male elements and the stencilled and painted common brown butterfly reflect birth and renewal. Silks and cottons are cyanotyped; the white images are the shadows of the actual leaves and grasses, indicating their former presence on the fabric surface, and so are symbolic of the past and death. The painted and appliqued leaf shapes represent the present; they have just fallen and have not fully merged with the quilt surface. The silks and cottons, so often regarded as delicate in nature, serve to remind us of the fragility of life. More often than not, the quilt will outlive its maker!

▶ Fragility
textile pigments, cotton and silk
fabrics;
stencilling, fabric painting,
cyanotype, hand applique,
machine pieced, hand quilted

Bronwyn Stafford-Barrett

●COLOUR IS A MAJOR
INFLUENCE FOR ME. I LOVE
THE STRONG CONTRASTS
YOU CAN SEE IN OUR
ENVIRONMENT●

SPRINGWOOD, NSW Quilting spreads from one end of Bronwyn's house to the other. She has lived in the Blue Mountains for seventeen years, and is very much influenced by the mountains and weather. Her life has been concerned with family and home. She has always had a needle in her hand, she's interested in art, and has combined these two in her quiltmaking.

I WAS WATCHING A FRIEND and her mother quilting. I had always sewed, made my own clothes, and when classes were starting up here the time was right for me to join. I had always been interested in art and liked fabrics, and I found them both in quilting. You have to really set up for painting, with space for an easel, paints and everything. Patchwork fitted in with being a mother.

I had a bad period for a while with five deaths in the family, my mother having major surgery and coping with a divorce as well. Quilting helped me through this very difficult time in my life. I don't know quite how I would have coped if I hadn't had the quilts to put my thoughts and feelings into. They took my mind from unhappy things and soothed me.

I have two daughters who are beginning to contribute their opinions on my quilts. They've started making small pieces. I suppose they've been influenced sufficiently to use fabrics and to look at designs for themselves. It's something that's grown with them in a minor way.

Colour is a major influence for me. I love the strong contrasts you can see in our environment. In my small quilt I've used contrast of colours to highlight the design of the blocks from the background.

Last year I was country member for the Quilters' Guild committee and this year I'm membership secretary. That's kept me in touch with other quilters. I visited people in Victoria and Queensland, which opened up a whole new range of contacts. Recently I've been teaching mildly intellectually impaired students at a special school. I took my quilts in to show them, and they were very interested. I'm also doing some quilts for my family at the moment, and when I've finished that I really want to extend to totally different areas of quilting.

▶ **Sampler in Points and Curves**
cottons;
hand pieced, hand quilted

Wendy Holland

**●I LIKE THE RANDOM
THINGS THAT HAPPEN WHEN
YOU DON'T PLAN TOO
CAREFULLY BUT ALLOW THE
PROCESS TO TAKE OVER —
THE DISCOVERY OF
RELATIONSHIPS●**

SYDNEY, NSW A fine arts
training and experience in
costumes provide a firm
foundation for Wendy's work in
textiles. She traces the influence of
fabrics and textile designs through
her working and creative life.
Wendy is a recognised quiltmaker,
having exhibited since 1980 and
participated in Craft Expo '84
and '85.

I ALWAYS LOVED TO DRAW and paint, and specialised in painting at art
school. I became attracted to decorative pattern and design in the
applied arts as well as to painting in the traditional sense. Certain marks
and shapes had power both in relationship to each other and in
repetition.

My fascination with Japanese surface design and other oriental and
ethnic textiles began at this time. I used to go down to Paddy's Market
from East Sydney Tech. and pick up lovely old pieces of fabric and
granny dresses for my own clothes. I was soon fixing things up to earn
a bit of money. You could still buy Japanese kimonos very cheaply
and I became adept at reassembling them into more saleable garments.
I ended up with a range of exotic scraps.

I worked in theatre wardrobe intermittently, and then did a Dip.
Ed. to maintain my teaching qualifications. When I was teaching, the
school did a production of *The Mikado* and the kids and I did all the
costumes. We printed and made them all up and I knew that this
interested me far more than teaching. It was a turning point: textiles,
printing, Japanese design — I left my job.

I got married and went to England in 1979. I happened to live
almost next to 'Strawberry Fayre', run by Alec and Jenny Hutchison
(she's now the president of the English Quilters' Guild). I was particularly drawn to the fabrics in the antique quilts they had there. It wasn't
long before I wanted to make a quilt myself with the old fabrics back
in Australia.

I like the random things that happen when you don't plan too
carefully but allow the process to take over — the discovery of relation-
ships. I think we have access to too many choices. When you limit
yourself to a bunch of scraps, you're forced to play around for the best
solution. The suitcase quilt was so small that I had trouble fitting
everything in. What wouldn't fit on around the edges went on to the
front. I wanted it to be fun to peer at up close, as well as having some
feeling of Australia.

▶ **First Fleet Flotsam**
cottons, embroidered pieces,
luminous plasticised material,
buttons, beads, diamantes,
clothing motifs;
machine pieced, hand
embroidered and quilted

Dianne Firth

❛I PREFER GEOMETRIC
FORMS AND A STRONG USE
OF COLOUR, PARTICULARLY
IN ASSOCIATION WITH LIGHT
AND SHADE EFFECTS❜

CANBERRA, ACT   Dianne lives in Canberra with her husband, John, and her three children. She maintains a dual career on the professional and domestic fronts and finds that quilting is a means of bringing the two interests together creatively. The qualities of light and colour in the shifting hues of sunset over the Brindabella Range have motivated her to produce her 'Attic Window' quilt.

I'M A LANDSCAPE ARCHITECT and teacher by profession, but I also have a love of domestic things. I like sewing and fabrics, and this has become an outlet for my landscaping work. In much of my designing, I'm picking up paving, landscaped things and putting them into fabrics. I look at garden design and the sky, particularly the sky, and translate it back into fabric art.

My first child was a boy and I guess I didn't make so many things for him, but the second was a girl and I made her a standard patched quilt. It was a simple square-patch baby's quilt which grew to a cot size when I needed it. A friend who was visiting thought I should see what *real* quilting was about and I was hooked!

I like putting fabric together in a functional way. I didn't have any lessons but began by looking in magazines and learning from experience. Then, when I was doing a triangle quilt, I was piecing every triangle together separately by hand. I found there was a better way to do it and realised the benefit of being taught, so I went to quilting classes.

Most of my quilts have been made for my family. The children have at least one quilt for their bed and I give them to relatives as gifts. I have also been involved in making quilts for schools and charity fundraising.

I prefer geometric forms and a strong use of colour, particularly in association with light and shade effects. There has to be an overall structure to satisfy me, but the most important things are the colour and light.

In 'Attic Window' the structure is a device to show the light quality of the Canberra sky at sunset. The screening breaks up the colours of the sky and the structure shows the shadows. When you look into the quilt you can see the variation of shadow in line with colour variations in the sky.

▶ **Sunset through the Attic Window**
cottons, polycottons;
hand pieced, hand quilted

Judith Watson

● THIS QUILT REPRESENTS
MY VIEW THAT 1788 WAS
THE BEGINNING OF A PERIOD
OF INCREDIBLE CHANGE IN
AUSTRALIA, RATHER THAN
THE BEGINNING OF
AUSTRALIA ITSELF ●

SYDNEY, NSW Judith settled on applique in her quilting style as a means of being more spontaneous and expressive. She develops a thematic concept in her designing and has found that it extends her appreciation of her subject matter. Her full-time occupation as a tutor in Econometrics limits her recreation time, but she continues quilting with support and impetus from her friendship quilt group.

I'M SURE I WAS GIVEN an early interest in fabrics by my grandmother, who provided packages of bridal fabric scraps for making dolls' clothes. I loved making things from the satins and lace, and it was always exciting to go through each new parcel. I became an early fabric hoarder.

My first quilt was a hexagon pattern with hundreds of paper templates. It was time-consuming and oh, so repetitive. I quickly developed an interest in applique and found it to be very expressive. It's faster and much more spectacular. You don't have to stick to the same shape over and over, and I find it easy to build up a picture.

I've had no formal lessons but I've picked up techniques from reading every available book and magazine on quilting. I'm involved with some talented quilters in a friendship group. Besides being fun, this is a wonderful way of widening one's horizons. It's been interesting to encounter so many patterns and fabrics, especially when they are different from those I would have chosen myself. This helps to open my eyes to new possibilities.

I guess it depends on the project, but I've got a feeling for solids — I make more of a statement of colour than of pattern. I'd love to get into dyeing shades within shades. I start with a theme and always have a basic plan, though I don't ever like to be tied to it.

I find I really enjoy all sorts of quilting, piecing, everything. These days it gets pushed to the back burner and then comes good again when I have the time. It's something my family lives with. They enjoy it, but it's a case of 'here comes mum and her mess again!'.

This quilt represents my view that 1788 was the beginning of a period of incredible change in Australia, rather than the beginning of Australia itself. I was thinking of Australian history, looking at symbols of the old culture and the new. Images of Cobb & Co. were quite unwieldy so they ended up as wheels and the convicts are shown as arrows, but the Aboriginal part of it was fun! I read lots of books on Aboriginal art and came to a better understanding of it. At Expo I was able to see wonderful Aboriginal paintings — so many interpretations of the same style! It was very beautiful.

▶ **1780s — Land of Change**
cottons, polycotton;
hand appliqued and hand quilted

Prue Socha

❛I LIKE A QUILT TO BE
FUNCTIONAL AND TO BE
EXPRESSIVE OF MY
RESPONSES❜

SYDNEY, NSW   Prue approaches her quiltmaking with a strong background in embroidery. Her quilts are an extension of her dyed and embroidered landscapes. She is committed to a very Australian sense in her work, evoking the colours and forms of the landscapes she loves so well.

MY GRANDMOTHER WAS a very good embroiderer but my mother, who was an architect, couldn't thread a needle. So when I was a little girl I was taught to embroider by June Scott-Stevenson, a wonderful woman who was my mother's friend. She was an early member of the Embroiderers' Guild and a well-known embroiderer of the day. Another of my mother's friends, Marion Hall-Best, had a wonderful design shop in Woollahra. She was the first person I knew who really understood colour and I was very influenced by this.

I joined the Embroiderers' Guild in 1969 and got my London City and Guilds Certificate of Hand Embroidery the next year. Since then I've been a tutor for the Embroiderers' Guild, the Crafts Council and Arts Council and various summer schools around Australia and New Zealand.

I love the Australian landscape and wanted a simple means of expressing it. I found I could get that with dye and stitching on embroidery canvas. For the past six years I've been interspersing my embroidery with making quilts. I like a quilt to be functional and to be expressive of my responses. I think it's terribly important that we develop our own style rather than reiterate a tradition from other countries. My first quilts showed a Japanese influence. I'd just been to Japan, and loved the people and the landscape. The rest have been Australian.

This quilt is one of a series inspired by a visit to Yulara in Central Australia. The colours of the quilt are the colours of the landscape. Embroidery adds to and emphasises the quilting, which was evoked by the Aboriginal rock paintings of the area. The french knots represent the ochre the Aborigines sprayed around their hands to leave an imprint on the rock surface.

▶ **Yulara**
cottons;
machine pieced, hand quilted
and embroidered

Wendy Saclier

●IT WAS THE BEGINNING OF
A NEW AND EXCITING PART
OF MY LIFE, AND HAS GIVEN
ME A GREAT DEAL OF
PLEASURE AND
SATISFACTION●

CANBERRA, ACT Wendy's crazy quilt combines traditional techniques and materials with random motifs of Australian life in Victorian times. Although she does not limit herself to the style, she has become known for her crazy patchworks. Wendy works as a speech pathologist with very young children. She also teaches and exhibits her quilts in Canberra and interstate.

Friends Judy Thompson and Margaret Rolfe introduced me to patchwork and quilting in 1976. It was the beginning of a new and exciting part of my life, and has given me a great deal of pleasure and satisfaction. Much of this has come from my involvement in the formation of the Patchwork Group (now Canberra Quilters) and the development of quilting friendships.

During the past twelve years I've explored many aspects of patchwork and quilting, from traditional to pieced pictures, machine embroidery and creating my own designs and techniques. As well as producing many quilts such as 'Australiana Victoriana' individually, I especially enjoy co-operative quiltmaking.

My first crazy quilt was created in 1979 as a result of being given a bag of exotic fabric scraps. Apart from a school embroidery sampler I had done very little needlework and had to teach myself from books as well as learning a great deal from my mother. She lived in Toowoomba at that time. I sent her the blocks, she did all the floral embroidery and sent it back. I did all the rest.

Seeing how beautiful the finished work was extended her even further; we have now made eleven quilts together in different styles, but mostly using applique techniques. It's lovely because we seem to like the same kinds of things and agree on colour and design.

Crazy patchwork is a Victorian style. In 'Australiana Victoriana' I wanted to include a range of things that were Australian in Victorian times, such as gold panning, tennis, fans and music of the time. I used exotic fabrics in deep, rich colours and embroidered the patches with appropriate pictorial and traditional motifs. I included Australian flowers and put my three cats in too. They're not particularly Victorian, but they do lend themselves to the design.

▶ **Australiana Victoriana**
silks, satins, velvet, brocade, lace, ribbon, braids and embroidery threads;
pressed applique, hand embroidered

Trudy Brodie

● MY WORK HAS BENEFITED GREATLY FROM TEACHING OTHERS THE JOY OF THIS COLOURFUL CRAFT ●

SYDNEY, NSW   Trudy's initial interest in embroidery led her to patchwork classes in America. When she returned to Australia she continued her interest in quiltmaking. She experiments with combinations of diamonds in the log cabin method and uses medallion structures in strong primary colours.

ALTHOUGH I BEGAN SEWING at an early age, I didn't begin patchwork and quilting until 1981 when I was living in Virginia, USA. I used to join other 'embassy wives' to learn different embroidery techniques. I'd only known the crewel embroidery we did at school, but here I saw ways of doing needlework I'd never known about before, and it was fascinating. A few months before we left I learnt patchwork from Mary Coyne Penders, a prominent teacher in the district. What appealed to me was making whole sections of colour with fabric in preference to using stitching.

On returning to Australia, I joined the Patchwork Group (now Canberra Quilters). This group provided new friendships and the enthusiasm to continue my new craft. I have exhibited in their annual exhibition every year since then and was newsletter editor for two years.

In 1983 I began to teach patchwork and quilting privately and to adult recreation classes at evening college. My work has benefited greatly from teaching others the joy of this colourful craft. I have entered quilts in several Royal Easter shows in Sydney and have won three first prizes.

In 1987 my family and I moved to Sydney. My work has continued to be mainly traditional in design, but occasionally breaking out to do something different. My current interest is in primary colours, medallion quilts and diamond designs.

My small quilt has been designed as a medallion quilt, the large diamond superimposed over a rectangle. The diamonds are assembled by using the log cabin method of construction. Two different widths of logs have been used in order to 'move' the centre of each diamond. I used a little bit of orange and yellow to let the light through and I'm pleased with the effect. I think I'm understanding colour much more now.

▶ **Diamonds Aglow**
cottons;
machine pieced and hand quilted

Greg Somerville

❛... QUILTMAKING ...
SEEMED TO BE A GOOD WAY
OF PUTTING MY IDEAS ON A
LARGER SCALE❜

WENTWORTH FALLS, NSW
Greg's lifelong relationship with textiles has found expression in his use of quiltmaking as a visual medium. His designs are graphic representations of a personal philosophy. He borrows Islamic and mandala motifs to represent his search for a deeper personal understanding which he explores during the reflective process of making the quilts.

WHEN I WAS FOUR YEARS OLD we lived with my grandmother. I spent most of my time with her and she taught me to knit and sew. I have grown up making things in crochet, with materials, and so on. When I was working at the Botanic Gardens I heard about quiltmaking and it seemed to be a good way of putting my ideas on a larger scale.

I started quiltmaking in 1978. It took me about two years to hand stitch and hand quilt my first one, working at it off and on. I did a course with Ruth Stonely in Tamworth and became inspired. I saw quiltmaking as something I wanted to begin as a career. I worked part-time and started to do a lot of work in sewing and quiltmaking. In 1986 I received a grant from the Australia Council to allow me to explore screenprinting and fabric painting in my quilts. Since then I've been using these techniques and a little airbrushing, cutting and adding these pieces to my quilts. It gives me a bit more control over what I can do instead of relying on what materials I can find.

For a long while I've been interested in Islamic mosaics and mandala patterns and it was this visual structure that started me in quiltmaking. It was a good way to show a mandala on a large scale. I use the mandala to represent the 'higher' self and usually I'm not aware of what meaning has been revealed until sometime later.

In this quilt the mandala, overlaid by the grid and with the 'paths' behind, is quite simple. The grid represents the trap of anxiety in our lives. The trap is to think there is only one path or way of doing things while, in fact, there are many possibilities. If you think there is only one right thing to do and only one right way to do it, decision-making becomes very hard because every decision is vital and you're anxious about making the right choice. If you have a hard and fast concept about the way your life should be, you're stuck. You're not open to new possibilities that may come along.

These are the 'paths'. Traditional people think of their life 'path' as their career, but I think of it more generally as whatever you're doing with your life. My quilt is a very simple representation of this concept.

▶ '... thinking there was only one way, I was stuck.'
cottons, polycottons;
machine pieced, hand quilted

Geraldine Couninis

● I LIKE THE IDEA OF THE
QUILTING PATTERN BEING
ALMOST INDEPENDENT OF
THE COLOUR IN A QUILT ●

PERTH, WA   Geraldine lives in
one of the oldest suburbs in Perth.
It's semi-bush and has a small,
village-like atmosphere which is
one of the reasons she likes it. Her
original career in teaching and
making ceramics has been taken
over by a love of textiles. This
comes through in her feeling for
quilts and costumes — two
consuming interests.

I TRAINED YEARS AGO in Tasmania as a secondary art teacher, and
taught in Australia then Scotland. Scotland was a bit of a fluke,
really. After about three years of teaching, it was suggested I do some
extra study. There was Edinburgh and ceramics or Manchester with
textiles. I went for the ceramics. I was lucky, because they had a one
year course for overseas students to work alongside their ceramics
students.

My father, grandfather and great-grandfather all had to do with
pottery and brickworks. As a little girl I spent a lot of time in the
pottery. I grew up with clay, mixing glazes, firing kilns, that sort of
thing.

Back in 1975 I was still in ceramics but had gone as far as I could
with it. Another lecturer said, 'Why not come into my section and
do textiles?'. I'd been feeling stuck because of some personal problems
and she suggested I do a workshop. So I went and for a week we sat
and talked textiles. That's when I really became interested. I saw the
book *America's Quilts and Coverlets* and for some reason, that book
became a lifebuoy. I designed a crib quilt, took it to work and talked
with people about it. I taught myself and became 'hooked'.

I like the idea of the quilting pattern being almost independent of
the colour in a quilt. I'd learnt how to use disperse dyes and liked the
fineness and sheen that gives a jewel-like effect from the polyester. And
I love what you can do with the paper; the way colours bleed back-
wards and forwards and the way you can let that dry, then work back
over the top so you get a kind of depth of field.

I get an idea and it develops in my mind for one or two weeks, even
a couple of months. Then, and only then, can I put it down on paper
but in my mind's eye I know just what I'm going to do.

I've built up quite a library of quilting and costume books. I love
reading and have always been fond of social history. In costumes I've
got everything: the textiles and the social history. I knew nothing
about costumes but quite suddenly that interest took off. I think
because it's tactile, really . . . and it's colour. They're the two strongest
features for me.

▶ **Fans II**
polyester and disperse dyes;
disperse dye technique,
hand quilted

Jennifer Lewis

● THE DIFFERENT TEXTURES AND COLOURS OF FABRICS AND THE SCOPE FOR INDIVIDUAL DESIGN APPEAL TO ME ●

MELBOURNE, VIC Jennifer has used images and fabrics associated with Balnarring beach where she has a family holiday house. Her quilt incorporates personal significance and her own designing to give a gentle layering of meaning. Her teaching philosophy spills over from her profession and parenting into her quiltmaking workshops where she encourages participants to recognise their own talents.

I HAVE BEEN FORTUNATE TO HAVE PARENTS and grandparents interested in the arts and creativity. My father fostered an awareness of the beauty of nature, music and the arts through his own talents and interests in these fields. My mother, having five daughters, fostered an interest in fabric and sewing. I suppose it's not surprising that I find the day too short to do all the things I would like to do, and have had to decide which is the most satisfying. I have chosen patchwork and quilting. The different textures and colours of fabrics and the scope for individual design appeal to me. I enjoy the way the personality of the quilter comes through the quilt — their choice of colour and design and the fascinating differences in the results.

I'm a kindergarten teacher. I particularly like the freedom of preschool children before they develop preconceived ideas. I don't like to direct people — I like to draw out of people their own talents. This is what I strive for with my own children, what I felt my parents did with me, and I think, what they had when they were growing up.

I recently travelled overseas to England and Europe. This gave me a sense of Australians building their own culture. Because we're removed from the strong European tradition, there seem to be more people 'doing their own thing' rather than buying antiques and living from cultural objects of the past. This awareness has made me more conscious of Australia's unique beauty.

My suitcase quilt was inspired by the foliage and flowers of Australian native plants and the pleasure of weekends at Balnarring beach. We have a holiday house there with coastal banksias and tea-trees in the garden, and enjoy family times with our daughter Hannah, who lives nearby.

Hannah does a lot of drawing and I drew inspiration from these and the paintings and prints of Margaret Preston, which I feel lend themselves very well to fabrics. I've used dyed homespun which I bought from Kerrin Daws at nearby Red Hill market, because of the beautifully muted colouring.

▶ **Balnarring Banksias**
cotton, dyed homespun;
hand piecing and applique

Fiona Gavens

❝I BEGAN LOOKING FOR A MORE DEMANDING AND INDIVIDUAL STYLE AND BEGAN THE TIGHT, CURVED PIECING, EXTENDING WHAT I HAD STARTED IN AUSTRALIA❞

WHITEMAN CREEK, NSW

Fiona has experimented with many approaches, both in making quilts and teaching her craft. Her distinctive style of curved piecing has developed strongly in the last three years, and has enabled her to suggest the moods of her environment, particularly the bush around her. She enjoys teaching advanced classes, choosing to expose her students to new ideas and techniques to encourage them in developing their own work.

I HAVE ALWAYS HAD A CRAFT ORIENTATION but it took me a long time to find the right medium.

Somewhat naively I started studying occupational therapy because of its craft orientation but dropped out after discovering it was about therapy rather than doing one's own craft! I then moved on to secretarial/administrative work. As Executive Secretary of the Craft Association of Victoria, and later as Project Officer with the Crafts Board, Australia Council, I was exposed to a wide variety of craftspeople — their work, philosophies and lifestyles. I met my husband (a potter) when he applied for a grant. He missed out on that and got me instead!

My first quilt was sewn by hand and, although it did not put me off patchwork, I vowed never to hand piece again! I have also hand quilted one bedspread, which made me determined to find a way to machine quilt (considered virtually impossible ten years ago). Then I discovered a book on Amish quilts. It was a revelation to see that quilts could be designed on a large scale and not broken up into blocks.

I received a Workshop Development grant from the Crafts Board in 1983 and it was a great boost to my morale as well as to my pocket. I bought a semi-industrial sewing machine and, as there are certain techniques I use now, I could not do without it.

I have won a number of prizes at exhibitions but the biggest thrill was having Stanthorpe Art Gallery (Queensland) buy a piece of my work. Another highlight was having a solo exhibition in Jamaica. I exhibited seventeen pieces, all made whilst living there (1986–1987). While in Jamaica I went to the Vermont Quilt Festival and came away feeling really challenged. I began looking for a more demanding and individual style and began the tight, curved piecing, extending what I had started in Australia. It does not relate to traditional blocks — the quilts fit together rather like a jigsaw. For a piece like 'Jacaranda Storm' I draw up a full-size cartoon and cut it up for pattern pieces. When piecing I often start a seam but leave it unfinished until a nearby related seam had been sewn. In this way I gradually build it up.

▶ Jacaranda Storm
cottons, polycottons, polyester;
machine pieced, machine quilted

Margaret Rolfe

●THE CHALLENGE AND
EXCITEMENT OF CREATING
ORIGINAL PATCHWORK
DESIGNS STILL REMAINS MY
CHIEF LOVE●

CANBERRA, ACT Margaret's pictorial blocks are well known both through her own quilts and through her books and magazine articles. Her interest in the history of Australian patchwork was recognised and supported by the Australia Council, enabling her to research and write a definitive work on the subject.

Although I was always interested in patchwork and quilting, if anyone had said to me thirteen years ago that it was to become a central part of my life, I would have laughed! Today, quilting has become my profession.

I started to learn the craft during a visit to the United States where I was taught the rudiments of the American approach. On returning to Australia I wanted to continue but there were no classes, almost no books and no help. I agonised over quilting — how exactly was it supposed to be done? The few books I could find seemed to contradict each other. Most of my learning had to come from experience — good old-fashioned trial and error. A friend returned from America with a similar enthusiasm, so we put a small ad in the paper and began what has become the Canberra Quilters. Others became interested in what I had learned and so the next step was to begin teaching.

I loved the traditional patterns, but began to feel that my quilting should reflect that I was an Australian. The wall hanging 'Australian Birds' was my first essay into putting my own environment into a quilt. I was particularly intrigued with the creative possibilities of pieced blocks, and designed a block for the Sturt's desert pea. Other wildflower designs soon developed. I also became interested in the history of patchwork in Australia. Both this interest and my designs for Australian patches led me to write a number of quilting books and subsequent articles for Australian and Japanese magazines.

The challenge and excitement of creating original patchwork designs still remains my chief love. I have developed a technique for putting together blocks which allows great freedom of design, yet simple piecing. I call it 'straight line patchwork' because the blocks can all be put together with seams of straight sewing. Seemingly complex designs become easy to sew and lots of fun to create.

The design for the galahs was inspired by the flocks of galahs which come every morning and sit on the electricity wires running along our backyard. I see the birds from my kitchen window and delight in their radiant colours. The name 'Galah Session' has an Australian colloquial meaning, being used to describe the sessions on outback radio phones when the women talk to each other.

▶ **The Galah Session**
cotton and polyester;
machine pieced, hand quilted
and embroidered

Barbara Macey

● THE LOG CABIN FORMAT
WAS EXCITING RIGHT FROM
THE START BECAUSE IT
SEEMED FULL OF 'HERE AND
NOW' IMAGERY ●

MELBOURNE, VIC   For some time Barbara has explored the log cabin technique, redefining and restructuring it to produce strong, graphic quilts. She has developed a technique which allows both quilting and piecing to be done in one operation. The abstract images she creates symbolise, in a simplified way, the order underlying our lives.

I BEGAN PATCHWORK IN 1972 but not with traditional quilts; nostalgia never interested me. The log cabin format was exciting right from the start because it seemed full of 'here and now' imagery. Thorough exploration of its intricacies has revealed a rich and flexible language capable of expressing a variety of concepts. This language allows a very personal translation of thoughts, observations and feelings into an abstract visual form.

Several themes have fascinated me, such as drought and returning, things I remember as a child, and the underground landscapes. The way things differ from what they appear to be on the surface is a major theme in my quilts. However, some quilts have no meaning other than as vehicles for exploring the visual language I work with. They are orderly yet complex, and produce patterns that are often ambiguous and many-layered, with a dazzling and hypnotic quality. I believe that simple elements organised into complex systems have a profound significance in the scheme of things; our lives revolve around them. Not being a mathematician I was surprised to realise that the systems I use are simply a way of presenting mathematical concepts in a visual form.

From childhood I was familiar with fabrics, threads and sewing machines, and after marriage acquired further skills in household sewing and home dressmaking and embroidery. Patchwork was a natural step from this background. The fabrics I use most often are ordinary plain cottons, wools and synthetics; very rarely prints. I do not look for fabrics that are luxurious or beautiful in themselves. The ones I use must have some attribute that creates or enhances the image I'm aiming for, and are often quite humble. Even the most unassuming fabric can have properties that inspire a unique quilt.

Australian quiltmakers owe a great deal to British and American traditions, but we can transform the various techniques to accommodate our personal feelings and observations. We can reflect who we are and where we live rather than reiterate the images of other times and places not appropriate here. I strongly believe that such individual efforts will lead to an Australian quilt tradition.

▶ **Blue Maze Quilt**
cottons, synthetic fabrics;
machine pieced

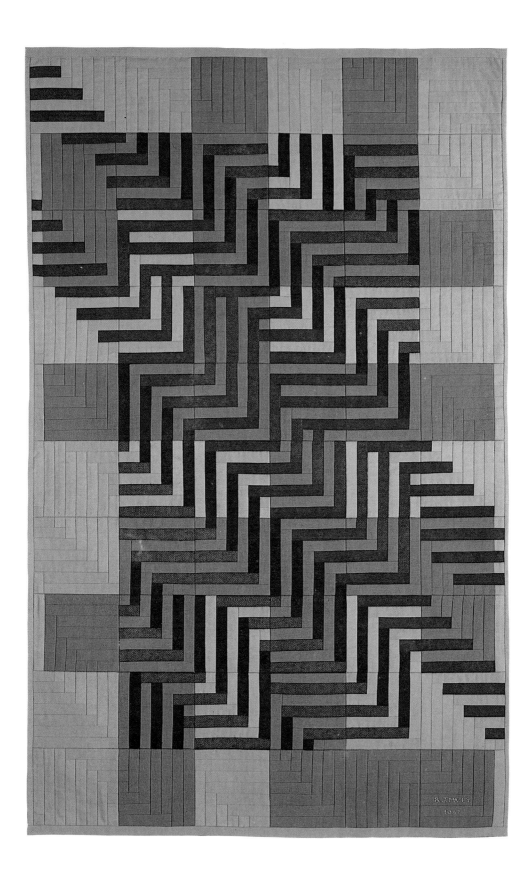

Noreen Dunn

❝I FEEL THAT EVERYTHING I DO NEEDS TO SHOW MY LIFE EXPERIENCE AND INDICATE THAT IT'S AN AUSTRALIAN EXPERIENCE❞

SYDNEY, NSW Enthusiasm has made Noreen very productive in the nine years since her first quilting class. Today she works in partnership on commissions and individually on her own quilts. She has travelled to many parts of Australia giving workshops and to the United States to develop her own expertise.

I FEEL THAT EVERYTHING I DO needs to show my life experience and indicate that it's an Australian experience. I've been working with colour and fabric for many years and it's the colour drawn from the Australian lifestyle that best expresses my feelings.

I got into quilting by a freak, really. My son gave me a six-week quilting course in 1979, because the course was on a Thursday and so was the football! That Mothers' Day present changed my life.

I've made quilts non-stop from the word go — jumped in feet first! So far I've made over two hundred quilts. I'm a genuine obsessive — I think I work ten days a week! I spread through the house a bit but I do have an area set up for quilting. It's a large workroom which was once a child's bedroom.

I'm involved in a partnership making quilts. My partner and I had been working together about one day a week just to be in touch with someone else who was quilting, and we started getting work. At about that time we went into Craft Expo together and that's when we formed the partnership.

As well as working on the commissions, we both make our own quilts. Mine are basically traditional. I really like vibrant colours and I'm very attracted to the way quilting changes the surface. The design of the quilting pattern is very important. It's been quite challenging to meet the demands of commissioned work but it's also good to take time off to do some for myself.

I like to feel proud of the work I've done so it needs to be well crafted. I feel strongly that design, workmanship and materials should be of the highest possible standard.

I think I'm influenced by really old quilts. I've seen quite a lot in America. In the future, I'd like to make fewer quilts with more time on each one. I'd like to make heirloom quilts.

▶ **Step and Stairs**
cotton fabrics;
strip pieced by machine,
hand quilted

Megan Terry

●I LIKE TO WORK ON
AUSTRALIAN THEMES IN MY
QUILTS . . . THEY ARE ALL
SUBJECTS DRAWN FROM
AREAS OF INTEREST I HAVE IN
THE AUSTRALIAN
LANDSCAPE●

MELBOURNE, VIC 'Cape Tribulation' is in the style of Megan's personal and descriptive quilts which relate to Australian landscapes. This is one of several styles of work she uses, the others being more traditional.

I BEGAN MY FIRST QUILT WHEN I WAS ONLY eighteen but didn't start seriously until the early 1970s. I was mostly interested in designs and didn't want to be conventional in what I made. I gave classes for several years. In 1978 my students and I had an exhibition of our work at my home. This was the beginning of what became the Australian Quilters' Association.

I like to work on Australian themes in my quilts. I've done an alpine meadow and Oodnadatta, a Coral Sea and others in my quilts. They are all subjects drawn from areas of interest I have in the Australian landscape.

At present I am pursuing my own quiltmaking interests: creative scrap bag (which I find exciting and mentally stimulating), some modern work with composition relating to Australia and its landscape, plus the occasional more traditional extravaganza which I find hard to resist.

Cape Tribulation is in the Daintree forest in far north Queensland. I made this quilt after I'd been in Port Douglas before it was 'developed'. I absolutely loved it!

This work depicts the rainforest, beach mangroves and ocean of this important part of the Daintree. I hadn't been to Cape Tribulation at that time, so I made it from my imagination. I've been along the coastline since then and it's much as I had envisaged it. I was thinking of conservation issues when I made it because the Bloomsfield track now cuts through that part of the rainforest like a great orange scar, creating huge ecological problems.

▶ **Cape Tribulation**
cottons, blends;
hand pieced, hand quilted
and beaded

Cynthia Morgan

❛I WAS LOOKING FOR A SOFTNESS IN MY WORK AND FOUND IT WHEN I LEARNT THE POLYCHROMATIC DYE TECHNIQUE WHERE YOU DON'T HAVE TO DEFINE AN EDGE TO THE SHAPES❜

CALOUNDRA, QLD Cynthia refined her response to dyes and dye technique over many years. Her watercolour style of dye application produces a hazy, gentle effect. She has been active in exhibiting her textiles for the past ten years and sometimes works to commission.

I'VE ALWAYS BEEN INTERESTED in textiles. My father was a draper and they were part of my childhood. As my own family grew up and I had more creative time, I started making woollen wall-hangings. I did a two-year visual arts course in Brisbane and then worked with another fibre artist in Scotland when I lived there. I came back to Australia and began screenprinting and embellishing the print with hand and machine embroidery. I introduced applique into my embellishment.

A screenprinted image is a harsh one. By embellishing and embroidering, I softened it. I was looking for a softness in my work and found it when I learnt the polychromatic dye technique where you don't have to define an edge to the shapes. I have two different ways of using dye — colouring fabric and dye painting. One colours the fabric and the other is descriptive. I enjoy the product of both and use them in different ways. Bought fabrics have a more defined edge and harsher finish. You can achieve much greater shading and subtlety with your own dyeing. I've recently been creating a lot of graduated colours in fabrics.

I've tried polysol dyeing on synthetics and I enjoy dye painting. 'Water Lilies' is dye painted using polychromatic dyeing with fibre reactive dyes. The design is drawn on a fine mesh polyester screen and dyes painted on the screen using watercolour techniques. I prevent areas from running into each other by drying the dye as I paint. When the painting is completed and dry, it is transferred to the fabric with a screenprinting technique. The dyes are released from the screen during the process and, after 'curing' overnight, the piece is steam pressed to fix the dye to the fibres. The chemicals are then washed out, leaving the fabric permanently dyed.

I've developed a 'Rainforest' series of work. 'Water Lilies' will, I think, be another series to come. I have wonderful childhood memories of gathering water lilies in a lagoon outside Rockhampton, which may be why I feel influenced by Monet. I saw his paintings of waterlilies in Paris and loved them.

▶ **Water Lilies**
cotton, fibre reactive dyes;
polychromatic dye technique,
hand and machine quilted

Trudy Billingsley

●I SEE COLOURS,
PARTICULARLY IN THE SKY. I
KEEP THEM IN MY MIND AND
PUT THEM BACK INTO THE
DIFFERENT THINGS I MAKE●

SYDNEY, NSW   Trudy's self-reliance and creative ingenuity, together with the influences of travel and other people, have collaborated to produce a distinctive style of quiltmaking. This evolution was evident in a retrospective exhibition of some fifty pieces at the Ku-ring-gai Community Arts Centre in Sydney, in 1987.

MY FATHER WAS A LIGHTHOUSE KEEPER, so there was always the lighthouse and a headland. We were isolated, with our nearest neighbours a boat trip away. We had no television, no electricity; we were self-sufficient and self-entertained.

Dad was a big influence. As a result of the war his nerves were in such a state that we had to be absolutely quiet. My twin brother had a heart condition and I think Mum decided to train him to enjoy quiet things. We used to make things, paint, draw and collect.

I trained as a nurse and travelled alone in different countries for nine years. After I was married we emigrated to Canada and lived there for four years. I saw an exhibition there called 'In Praise of Hands'. There were all sorts of things on exhibition but I became particularly interested in the quilts. They were friendship and group quilts and I liked the warmth of the community aspect and their tactile quality. That's when I began making quilts. We returned to Australia and I started teaching traditional patchwork and quilting classes.

My husband travelled a lot and I was at home with the kids and getting sick of it. He suggested that I organise a trip of my own while he looked after them. I think he thought I'd go up to the mountains for a few days. I went out and arranged it all and came back and said, 'I'm going to Nantucket.' I travelled to Toronto to meet the Mennonite Quilters and do a ten-day workshop with Virginia Avery. When I came back I conducted a few workshops for the Quilters' Guild and helped to set up the St Ives group.

We moved to Boston and I went to workshops with many of the well-known quilters including Nancy Halpern and Rhoda Cohen. That's where I changed my style. My enjoyment of drawing came out and I began doing landscapes — playing with colour and design. I drew from memory and then went to the library and researched paintings on similar themes. Then I'd collect fabrics with the movement or mood I wanted.

'Summer Days' developed from memories of a trip we made during 1986 to Bourke. I wanted to show the brilliance of Australia's landscape colours, our clear skies and rusty coloured terrain.

▶ Summer Days
assorted fabrics, appliqued fabrics, appliqued on surface, shadow work, painted landscapes; hand and machine pieced, hand quilted

Ann Haddad

●MY WORK REFLECTS MY
OBVIOUS PREFERENCE FOR
TRADITIONAL PATTERNS. I
LIKE TO EXPERIMENT WITH
THE TRADITIONAL SHAPES,
BUT USING GEOMETRIC
RATHER THAN CURVED
PIECES●

CANBERRA, ACT   Ann's preference for traditional quiltmaking is enlivened by her individualised designs. She attends workshops to extend her skills and enjoys her association with other quilters through meetings and friendship quilt groups.

As a small child my mother introduced me to sewing and needlework and her precious bag of scraps, and I've been interested in fabric ever since. My introduction to patchwork and quilting came in 1981 when I visited an exhibition by the Patchwork Group (now Canberra Quilters) in Canberra. I'd done a little bit of hexagon patchwork but I wasn't terribly interested in it. However, my interest was sparked when I saw all the possibilities of using fabrics in those exhibition quilts.

I attended basic classes in 1982 and since then have completed bedsize quilts and wall-hangings, and participated in many friendship quilts. I have attended a number of workshops and have enjoyed learning different techniques. I tend to look out for a remark that spins my thinking off into something relevant to my work. This might be a comment about use of colour or a greater emphasis on design — whatever extends my thinking at that time. I enjoy experimenting with colour. In this particular quilt I've used colours that remind me of sunsets in the outback and put them in a traditional block design.

I think it's important to know the conventional rules of patchwork and quilting, but not necessarily to follow them. You need to be mindful of your purpose in making the quilt; if it's functional you should follow traditional instructions to make it practical, but if it's a wall-hanging you can be more flexible. You can do anything with patchwork — you can use the basic fabric, paint it or decorate it as you want.

My work reflects my obvious preference for traditional patterns. I like to experiment with the traditional shapes, but using geometric rather than curved pieces.

I'm basically still interested in making bed quilts, although at the moment I'm making banners from old vestments for Marist College here in Canberra. I spend most of my free time quilting. I've been granted a study because I made such a mess in the rest of the house! I store my fabrics in an old wooden post office cupboard with twenty-eight deep pigeon-holes. Its perfect for storing fabrics and looks so beautiful.

▶ Jewels in the Attic
cotton;
handpieced, machine pieced,
hand quilted

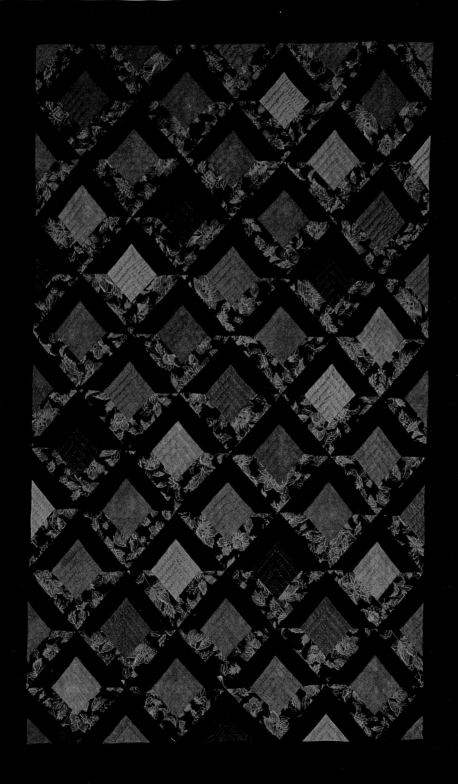

Jan Irvine

❛I BELIEVE THAT PERSONAL
EXPRESSION IS THE POINT OF
CREATIVE ACTIVITY, BE THAT
A MODEST QUALIFICATION
OR A DRIVING PASSION IN
LIFE❜

SYDNEY, NSW Jan was challenged by a dual opportunity to develop her own work for exhibition and to become involved in arts administration. She chose to do both and has run the two interests concurrently, feeling that one activity fuels the other. Her individual style of working has found expression by airbrushing dye on to whole cloth which she embellishes with stitching. Her work appears contemporary while deeply entrenched in the ancient tradition of stitching.

I WORKED AS AN OCCASIONAL INSTRUCTOR in fabric skills over a period of four years with a group of Pitjantjatjara women in north-west South Australia. These strong and forthright women have had a deep and lasting influence on me.

When my daughter began school I was 'grounded' in the city. I began piecing fabrics as an enjoyable pastime, an extension of using the tie-dyed and printed scraps in our desert workshops. This kind of recreational enjoyment is an inheritance from my family. Both my parents are ingenious at making things.

When I came back to town and found images in my mind, I translated them through fabrics, the most comfortable medium I knew. I began piecing my imagery but always looking for subtleties difficult to achieve with a constructed line. I tried overlays of chiffon to build up images and, while it allowed a much greater freedom and delicacy of colour and form, there was still the limitation of the defined edge.

Later, I moved to Sydney and had access to an airbrush. Thanks to support from the Australia Council, I have been able to develop my technique. By stretching my cloth and airbrushing dye through stencils I can now create any effect I choose. The technique provides such scope that I feel there's a lifetime of possibility in it.

I create visual images and then stitch them, adding a deeply satisfying dimension — the indenting of the surface, the immersion into an ancient practice and the pure pleasure of seeing the subtle play of light on the surface. My imagery has a personal meaning but I don't expect others to see it. It's appropriate that they respond directly to what they see and find their own interpretation.

Technically I draw on the traditions of quilting and embroidery but I use the stitch for its design purpose of embossing and marking the surface. I enjoy a fully stitched surface for its drape-like quality and the charm of the stitch itself. I refer to these works as 'stitched textiles' to encourage people to register them as a visual work before they see technique.

You often hear reference to the 'quilt as an art form'. The demarcation between art and craft is tiresome to me. I believe that personal expression is the point of creative activity, be that a modest qualification or a driving passion in life.

▶ **Seashore**
silk;
airbrush dyed, hand stitched

Contact Addresses

The Quilters' Guild Inc.
PO Box 654
Neutral Bay NSW 2089

Canberra Quilters Inc.
PO Box 29
Jamison Centre ACT 2614

Australian Quilters' Association
PO Box 497
Hawthorn Vic 3122

Quilters' Guild of South Australia Inc.
PO Box 993
Norwood SA 5067

The Western Australian Quilters'
Association Inc.
PO Box 188
Subiaco WA 6008

2Q — Queensland Quilters
GPO Box 2841
Brisbane Qld 4001

Alice Springs Quilting Group
PO Box 3301
Alice Springs NT 5750

Darwin Patchworkers and
Quilters
PO Box 518
Humpty Doo NT 5791

Tasmanian Quilting Guild
PO Box 1217
Gravelly Beach Tas 7251

Photographic Credits

Douglass Baglin   46, 70
Moira Burke   42
Chris Eade   72
Andrew Eggleston   84
Irvine Green   76
Z. Gruzauskas   82

Robert Heazlewood   10
Heidi Schmidt Studios   62
Herrain Photo Studio   74
Martin Jorgensen   88
Michael Kluvanek   50
Arné Knowland   40

David Meldrum   86
Michael Thorne Enterprises   26
Betty Neyland   36
Manual Patty   44
Sylvie Picot   34, 54, 66
M. Wert   24